KEEP IT SECRET
FROM FRIENDS AND FAMILY EDITION
Journal

Activinotes

Activinotes

DAILY JOURNALS, PLANNERS, NOTEBOOKS AND OTHER BLANK BOOKS

Copyright 2016

Password Journal

Account Name: _____

Website : _____

User I.D. : _____

Email Used : _____

Password : _____

Password Change	Date

Notes

Account Name: _____

Website : _____

User I.D. : _____

Email Used : _____

Password : _____

Password Change	Date

Account Name: _____

Website : _____

User I.D. : _____

Email Used : _____

Password : _____

Password Change	Date

Notes

Notes

Password Journal

Notes

Account Name: _____

Website : _____

User I.D. : _____

Email Used : _____

Password : _____

Password Change	Date

Account Name: _____

Website : _____

User I.D. : _____

Email Used : _____

Password : _____

Password Change	Date

Account Name: _____

Website : _____

User I.D. : _____

Email Used : _____

Password : _____

Password Change	Date

Notes

Notes

Password Journal

Notes

Account Name: _____

Website : _____

User I.D. : _____

Email Used : _____

Password : _____

Password Change	Date

Account Name: _____

Website : _____

User I.D. : _____

Email Used : _____

Password : _____

Password Change	Date

Account Name: _____

Website : _____

User I.D. : _____

Email Used : _____

Password : _____

Password Change	Date

Notes

Notes

Password Journal

Notes

Account Name: _____

Website : _____

User I.D. : _____

Email Used : _____

Password : _____

Password Change	Date

Account Name: _____

Website : _____

User I.D. : _____

Email Used : _____

Password : _____

Password Change	Date

Account Name: _____

Website : _____

User I.D. : _____

Email Used : _____

Password : _____

Password Change	Date

Notes

Notes

Password Journal

Notes

Account Name: _____

Website : _____

User I.D. : _____

Email Used : _____

Password : _____

Password Change	Date

Account Name: _____

Website : _____

User I.D. : _____

Email Used : _____

Password : _____

Password Change	Date

Account Name: _____

Website : _____

User I.D. : _____

Email Used : _____

Password : _____

Password Change	Date

Notes

Notes

Password Journal

Notes

Account Name: _____

Website : _____

User I.D. : _____

Email Used : _____

Password : _____

Password Change	Date

Account Name: _____

Website : _____

User I.D. : _____

Email Used : _____

Password : _____

Password Change	Date

Account Name: _____

Website : _____

User I.D. : _____

Email Used : _____

Password : _____

Password Change	Date

Notes

Notes

Password Journal

Account Name: _____

Website : _____

User I.D. : _____

Email Used : _____

Password : _____

Password Change	Date

Notes

Account Name: _____

Website : _____

User I.D. : _____

Email Used : _____

Password : _____

Password Change	Date

Account Name: _____

Website : _____

User I.D. : _____

Email Used : _____

Password : _____

Password Change	Date

Notes

Notes

Password Journal

Account Name: _____

Website : _____

User I.D. : _____

Email Used : _____

Password : _____

Password Change	Date

Notes

Account Name: _____

Website : _____

User I.D. : _____

Email Used : _____

Password : _____

Password Change	Date

Account Name: _____

Website : _____

User I.D. : _____

Email Used : _____

Password : _____

Password Change	Date

Notes

Notes

Password Journal

Account Name: _____

Website : _____

User I.D. : _____

Email Used : _____

Password : _____

Password Change	Date

Notes

Account Name: _____

Website : _____

User I.D. : _____

Email Used : _____

Password : _____

Password Change	Date

Account Name: _____

Website : _____

User I.D. : _____

Email Used : _____

Password : _____

Password Change	Date

Notes

Notes

Password Journal

Account Name: _____

Website : _____

User I.D. : _____

Email Used : _____

Password : _____

Password Change	Date

Notes

Account Name: _____

Website : _____

User I.D. : _____

Email Used : _____

Password : _____

Password Change	Date

Account Name: _____

Website : _____

User I.D. : _____

Email Used : _____

Password : _____

Password Change	Date

Notes

Notes

Password Journal

Account Name: _____

Website : _____

User I.D. : _____

Email Used : _____

Password : _____

Password Change	Date

Notes

Account Name: _____

Website : _____

User I.D. : _____

Email Used : _____

Password : _____

Password Change	Date

Account Name: _____

Website : _____

User I.D. : _____

Email Used : _____

Password : _____

Password Change	Date

Notes

Notes

Password Journal

Account Name: _____

Website : _____

User I.D. : _____

Email Used : _____

Password : _____

Password Change	Date

Notes

Account Name: _____

Website : _____

User I.D. : _____

Email Used : _____

Password : _____

Password Change	Date

Account Name: _____

Website : _____

User I.D. : _____

Email Used : _____

Password : _____

Password Change	Date

Notes

Notes

Password Journal

Account Name: _____

Website : _____

User I.D. : _____

Email Used : _____

Password : _____

Password Change	Date

Notes

Account Name: _____

Website : _____

User I.D. : _____

Email Used : _____

Password : _____

Password Change	Date

Account Name: _____

Website : _____

User I.D. : _____

Email Used : _____

Password : _____

Password Change	Date

Notes

Notes

Password Journal

Notes

Account Name: _____

Website : _____

User I.D. : _____

Email Used : _____

Password : _____

Password Change	Date

Account Name: _____

Website : _____

User I.D. : _____

Email Used : _____

Password : _____

Password Change	Date

Account Name: _____

Website : _____

User I.D. : _____

Email Used : _____

Password : _____

Password Change	Date

Notes

Notes

Password Journal

Account Name: _____

Website : _____

User I.D. : _____

Email Used : _____

Password : _____

Password Change	Date

Notes

Account Name: _____

Website : _____

User I.D. : _____

Email Used : _____

Password : _____

Password Change	Date

Account Name: _____

Website : _____

User I.D. : _____

Email Used : _____

Password : _____

Password Change	Date

Notes

Notes

Password Journal

Notes

Account Name: _____

Website : _____

User I.D. : _____

Email Used : _____

Password : _____

Password Change	Date

Account Name: _____

Website : _____

User I.D. : _____

Email Used : _____

Password : _____

Password Change	Date

Account Name: _____

Website : _____

User I.D. : _____

Email Used : _____

Password : _____

Password Change	Date

Notes

Notes

Password Journal

Account Name: _____

Website : _____

User I.D. : _____

Email Used : _____

Password : _____

Password Change	Date

Notes

Account Name: _____

Website : _____

User I.D. : _____

Email Used : _____

Password : _____

Password Change	Date

Account Name: _____

Website : _____

User I.D. : _____

Email Used : _____

Password : _____

Password Change	Date

Notes

Notes

Password Journal

Account Name: _____

Website : _____

User I.D. : _____

Email Used : _____

Password : _____

Password Change	Date

Notes

Account Name: _____

Website : _____

User I.D. : _____

Email Used : _____

Password : _____

Password Change	Date

Account Name: _____

Website : _____

User I.D. : _____

Email Used : _____

Password : _____

Password Change	Date

Notes

Notes

Password Journal

Notes

Account Name: _____

Website : _____

User I.D. : _____

Email Used : _____

Password : _____

Password Change	Date

Account Name: _____

Website : _____

User I.D. : _____

Email Used : _____

Password : _____

Password Change	Date

Account Name: _____

Website : _____

User I.D. : _____

Email Used : _____

Password : _____

Password Change	Date

Notes

Notes

Password Journal

Notes

Account Name: _____

Website : _____

User I.D. : _____

Email Used : _____

Password : _____

Password Change	Date

Account Name: _____

Website : _____

User I.D. : _____

Email Used : _____

Password : _____

Password Change	Date

Account Name: _____

Website : _____

User I.D. : _____

Email Used : _____

Password : _____

Password Change	Date

Notes

Notes

Password Journal

Account Name: _____

Website : _____

User I.D. : _____

Email Used : _____

Password : _____

Password Change	Date

Notes

Account Name: _____

Website : _____

User I.D. : _____

Email Used : _____

Password : _____

Password Change	Date

Account Name: _____

Website : _____

User I.D. : _____

Email Used : _____

Password : _____

Password Change	Date

Notes

Notes

Password Journal

Notes

Account Name: _____

Website : _____

User I.D. : _____

Email Used : _____

Password : _____

Password Change	Date

Account Name: _____

Website : _____

User I.D. : _____

Email Used : _____

Password : _____

Password Change	Date

Account Name: _____

Website : _____

User I.D. : _____

Email Used : _____

Password : _____

Password Change	Date

Notes

Notes

Password Journal

Account Name: _____

Website : _____

User I.D. : _____

Email Used : _____

Password : _____

Password Change	Date

Notes

Account Name: _____

Website : _____

User I.D. : _____

Email Used : _____

Password : _____

Password Change	Date

Account Name: _____

Website : _____

User I.D. : _____

Email Used : _____

Password : _____

Password Change	Date

Notes

Notes

Password Journal

Account Name: _____

Website : _____

User I.D. : _____

Email Used : _____

Password : _____

Password Change	Date

Notes

Account Name: _____

Website : _____

User I.D. : _____

Email Used : _____

Password : _____

Password Change	Date

Account Name: _____

Website : _____

User I.D. : _____

Email Used : _____

Password : _____

Password Change	Date

Notes

Notes

Password Journal

Account Name: _____

Website : _____

User I.D. : _____

Email Used : _____

Password : _____

Password Change	Date

Notes

Account Name: _____

Website : _____

User I.D. : _____

Email Used : _____

Password : _____

Password Change	Date

Account Name: _____

Website : _____

User I.D. : _____

Email Used : _____

Password : _____

Password Change	Date

Notes

Notes

Password Journal

Account Name: _____

Website : _____

User I.D. : _____

Email Used : _____

Password : _____

Password Change	Date

Notes

Account Name: _____

Website : _____

User I.D. : _____

Email Used : _____

Password : _____

Password Change	Date

Account Name: _____

Website : _____

User I.D. : _____

Email Used : _____

Password : _____

Password Change	Date

Notes

Notes

Password Journal

Account Name: _____

Website : _____

User I.D. : _____

Email Used : _____

Password : _____

Password Change	Date

Notes

Account Name: _____

Website : _____

User I.D. : _____

Email Used : _____

Password : _____

Password Change	Date

Account Name: _____

Website : _____

User I.D. : _____

Email Used : _____

Password : _____

Password Change	Date

Notes

Notes

Password Journal

Account Name: _____

Website : _____

User I.D. : _____

Email Used : _____

Password : _____

Password Change	Date

Notes

Account Name: _____

Website : _____

User I.D. : _____

Email Used : _____

Password : _____

Password Change	Date

Account Name: _____

Website : _____

User I.D. : _____

Email Used : _____

Password : _____

Password Change	Date

Notes

Notes

Password Journal

Account Name: _____

Website : _____

User I.D. : _____

Email Used : _____

Password : _____

Password Change	Date

Notes

Account Name: _____

Website : _____

User I.D. : _____

Email Used : _____

Password : _____

Password Change	Date

Account Name: _____

Website : _____

User I.D. : _____

Email Used : _____

Password : _____

Password Change	Date

Notes

Notes

Password Journal

Account Name: _____

Website : _____

User I.D. : _____

Email Used : _____

Password : _____

Password Change	Date

Notes

Account Name: _____

Website : _____

User I.D. : _____

Email Used : _____

Password : _____

Password Change	Date

Account Name: _____

Website : _____

User I.D. : _____

Email Used : _____

Password : _____

Password Change	Date

Notes

Notes

Password Journal

Account Name: _____

Website : _____

User I.D. : _____

Email Used : _____

Password : _____

Password Change	Date

Notes

Account Name: _____

Website : _____

User I.D. : _____

Email Used : _____

Password : _____

Password Change	Date

Account Name: _____

Website : _____

User I.D. : _____

Email Used : _____

Password : _____

Password Change	Date

Notes

Notes

Password Journal

Notes

Account Name: _____

Website : _____

User I.D. : _____

Email Used : _____

Password : _____

Password Change	Date

Account Name: _____

Website : _____

User I.D. : _____

Email Used : _____

Password : _____

Password Change	Date

Account Name: _____

Website : _____

User I.D. : _____

Email Used : _____

Password : _____

Password Change	Date

Notes

Notes

Password Journal

Account Name: _____

Website : _____

User I.D. : _____

Email Used : _____

Password : _____

Password Change	Date

Notes

Account Name: _____

Website : _____

User I.D. : _____

Email Used : _____

Password : _____

Password Change	Date

Notes

Account Name: _____

Website : _____

User I.D. : _____

Email Used : _____

Password : _____

Password Change	Date

Notes

Password Journal

Account Name: _____

Website : _____

User I.D. : _____

Email Used : _____

Password : _____

Password Change	Date

Notes

Account Name: _____

Website : _____

User I.D. : _____

Email Used : _____

Password : _____

Password Change	Date

Account Name: _____

Website : _____

User I.D. : _____

Email Used : _____

Password : _____

Password Change	Date

Notes

Notes

Password Journal

Account Name: _____

Website : _____

User I.D. : _____

Email Used : _____

Password : _____

Password Change	Date

Notes

Account Name: _____

Website : _____

User I.D. : _____

Email Used : _____

Password : _____

Password Change	Date

Account Name: _____

Website : _____

User I.D. : _____

Email Used : _____

Password : _____

Password Change	Date

Notes

Notes

Password Journal

Account Name: _____

Website : _____

User I.D. : _____

Email Used : _____

Password : _____

Password Change	Date

Notes

Account Name: _____

Website : _____

User I.D. : _____

Email Used : _____

Password : _____

Password Change	Date

Account Name: _____

Website : _____

User I.D. : _____

Email Used : _____

Password : _____

Password Change	Date

Notes

Notes

Password Journal

Account Name: _____

Website : _____

User I.D. : _____

Email Used : _____

Password : _____

Password Change	Date

Account Name: _____

Website : _____

User I.D. : _____

Email Used : _____

Password : _____

Password Change	Date

Account Name: _____

Website : _____

User I.D. : _____

Email Used : _____

Password : _____

Password Change	Date

Notes

Notes

Password Journal

Account Name: _____

Website : _____

User I.D. : _____

Email Used : _____

Password : _____

Password Change	Date

Notes

Account Name: _____

Website : _____

User I.D. : _____

Email Used : _____

Password : _____

Password Change	Date

Notes

Account Name: _____

Website : _____

User I.D. : _____

Email Used : _____

Password : _____

Password Change	Date

Notes

Password Journal

Account Name: _____
Website : _____
User I.D. : _____
Email Used : _____
Password : _____

Password Change	Date

Notes

Account Name: _____
Website : _____
User I.D. : _____
Email Used : _____
Password : _____

Password Change	Date

Account Name: _____
Website : _____
User I.D. : _____
Email Used : _____
Password : _____

Password Change	Date

Notes

Notes

Password Journal

Account Name: _____

Website : _____

User I.D. : _____

Email Used : _____

Password : _____

Password Change	Date

Notes

Account Name: _____

Website : _____

User I.D. : _____

Email Used : _____

Password : _____

Password Change	Date

Account Name: _____

Website : _____

User I.D. : _____

Email Used : _____

Password : _____

Password Change	Date

Notes

Notes

Password Journal

Account Name: _____

Website : _____

User I.D. : _____

Email Used : _____

Password : _____

Password Change	Date

Notes

Account Name: _____

Website : _____

User I.D. : _____

Email Used : _____

Password : _____

Password Change	Date

Notes

Account Name: _____

Website : _____

User I.D. : _____

Email Used : _____

Password : _____

Password Change	Date

Notes

Password Journal

Notes

Account Name: _____

Website : _____

User I.D. : _____

Email Used : _____

Password : _____

Password Change	Date

Account Name: _____

Website : _____

User I.D. : _____

Email Used : _____

Password : _____

Password Change	Date

Account Name: _____

Website : _____

User I.D. : _____

Email Used : _____

Password : _____

Password Change	Date

Notes

Notes

Password Journal

Notes

Account Name: _____

Website : _____

User I.D. : _____

Email Used : _____

Password : _____

Password Change	Date

Account Name: _____

Website : _____

User I.D. : _____

Email Used : _____

Password : _____

Password Change	Date

Account Name: _____

Website : _____

User I.D. : _____

Email Used : _____

Password : _____

Password Change	Date

Notes

Notes

Password Journal

Notes

Account Name: _____

Website : _____

User I.D. : _____

Email Used : _____

Password : _____

Password Change	Date

Account Name: _____

Website : _____

User I.D. : _____

Email Used : _____

Password : _____

Password Change	Date

Account Name: _____

Website : _____

User I.D. : _____

Email Used : _____

Password : _____

Password Change	Date

Notes

Notes

Password Journal

Account Name: _____

Website : _____

User I.D. : _____

Email Used : _____

Password : _____

Password Change	Date

Notes

Account Name: _____

Website : _____

User I.D. : _____

Email Used : _____

Password : _____

Password Change	Date

Account Name: _____

Website : _____

User I.D. : _____

Email Used : _____

Password : _____

Password Change	Date

Notes

Notes

Password Journal

Notes

Account Name: _____

Website : _____

User I.D. : _____

Email Used : _____

Password : _____

Password Change	Date

Account Name: _____

Website : _____

User I.D. : _____

Email Used : _____

Password : _____

Password Change	Date

Account Name: _____

Website : _____

User I.D. : _____

Email Used : _____

Password : _____

Password Change	Date

Notes

Notes

Password Journal

Account Name: _____

Website : _____

User I.D. : _____

Email Used : _____

Password : _____

Password Change	Date

Notes

Account Name: _____

Website : _____

User I.D. : _____

Email Used : _____

Password : _____

Password Change	Date

Account Name: _____

Website : _____

User I.D. : _____

Email Used : _____

Password : _____

Password Change	Date

Notes

Notes

Password Journal

Account Name: _____

Website : _____

User I.D. : _____

Email Used : _____

Password : _____

Password Change	Date

Notes

Account Name: _____

Website : _____

User I.D. : _____

Email Used : _____

Password : _____

Password Change	Date

Account Name: _____

Website : _____

User I.D. : _____

Email Used : _____

Password : _____

Password Change	Date

Notes

Notes

Password Journal

Account Name: _____

Website : _____

User I.D. : _____

Email Used : _____

Password : _____

Password Change	Date

Notes

Account Name: _____

Website : _____

User I.D. : _____

Email Used : _____

Password : _____

Password Change	Date

Account Name: _____

Website : _____

User I.D. : _____

Email Used : _____

Password : _____

Password Change	Date

Notes

Notes

Password Journal

Account Name: _____

Website : _____

User I.D. : _____

Email Used : _____

Password : _____

Password Change	Date

Notes

Account Name: _____

Website : _____

User I.D. : _____

Email Used : _____

Password : _____

Password Change	Date

Account Name: _____

Website : _____

User I.D. : _____

Email Used : _____

Password : _____

Password Change	Date

Notes

Notes

Password Journal

Account Name: _____

Website : _____

User I.D. : _____

Email Used : _____

Password : _____

Password Change	Date

Notes

Account Name: _____

Website : _____

User I.D. : _____

Email Used : _____

Password : _____

Password Change	Date

Account Name: _____

Website : _____

User I.D. : _____

Email Used : _____

Password : _____

Password Change	Date

Notes

Notes

Notes

www.ingramcontent.com/pod-product-compliance
Lightning Source LLC
Chambersburg PA
CBHW081334090426
42737CB00017B/3145